Animal Fare

Animal Fare

POEMS BY

JANE YOLEN

ILLUSTRATED BY

JANET STREET

HARCOURT BRACE & COMPANY

San Diego   New York   London

Requests for permission to make copies of any part of the work
should be mailed to: Permissions Department,
Harcourt Brace & Company, 8th Floor,
Orlando, Florida 32887.

Library of Congress Cataloging-in-Publication Data
Yolen, Jane.
Animal fare: poems by Jane Yolen;
illustrated by Janet Street. — 1st ed.
p.   cm.
Summary: A collection of sixteen nonsense poems about the
anteloop, the sprinkler spaniel, the rhinocerworse,
and other fantastic animals.
ISBN 0-15-203550-8
1. Animals — Juvenile poetry. 2. Nonsense verses, American.
3. Children's poetry, American. [1. Animals, Mythical — Poetry.
2. Nonsense verses. 3. American poetry.]
I. Street, Janet, ill. II. Title.
PS3575.043A83   1994
811'.54 — dc20   92-44931

Printed in Singapore

First edition
A B C D E

For Louise and Rubin with love
—*J. Y.*

For Lynne, Hans, and Nick
—*J. S.*

The paintings in this book were done in watercolors on 140-lb.
Fabriano cold-press watercolor paper.
The display type was set in Ozwald by the
Photocomposition Center,
Harcourt Brace & Company, San Diego, California.
The text type was set in Leawood Book by Thompson Type,
San Diego, California.
Color separations by Bright Arts, Ltd., Singapore
Printed and bound by Tien Wah Press, Singapore
Production supervision by Warren Wallerstein
and David Hough
Designed by Lori J. McThomas

Contents

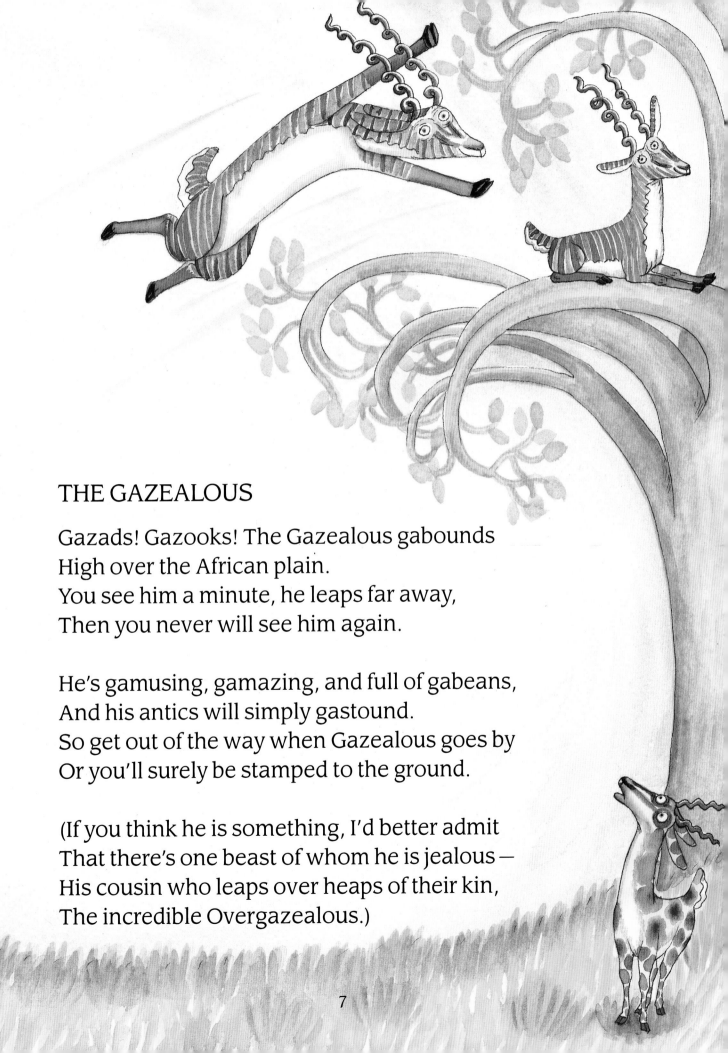

THE GAZEALOUS

Gazads! Gazooks! The Gazealous gabounds
High over the African plain.
You see him a minute, he leaps far away,
Then you never will see him again.

He's gamusing, gamazing, and full of gabeans,
And his antics will simply gastound.
So get out of the way when Gazealous goes by
Or you'll surely be stamped to the ground.

(If you think he is something, I'd better admit
That there's one beast of whom he is jealous —
His cousin who leaps over heaps of their kin,
The incredible Overgazealous.)

THE WHEREWOLF & KIN*

The wherewolf lives in Transylvania,
The whenwolf lives in Ruritania,
The whowolf lives in Pennsylvania.
They whowl the whole night long.

The whywolf lives in old Rumania,
The whatwolf lives in Mauritania,
And each one drives men quite insania
With his whild and whorrible song.

WHY?

WHERE?

*With whelp from Nancy Fowler, a whell-known Slavic scholar

8

9

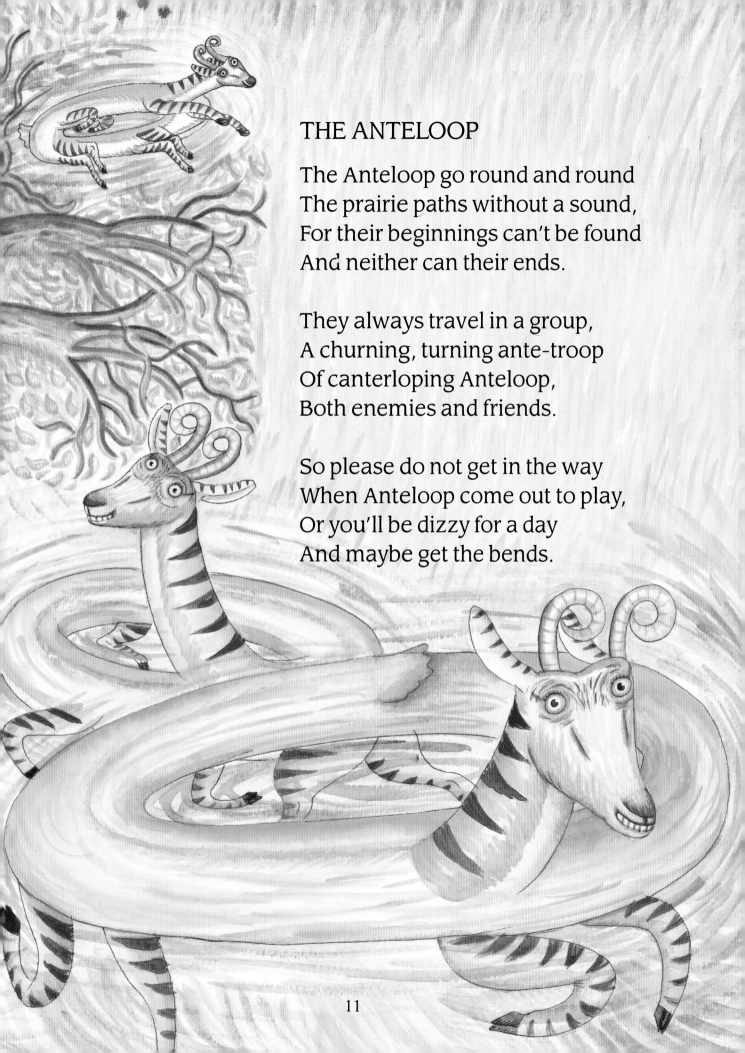

THE ANTELOOP

The Anteloop go round and round
The prairie paths without a sound,
For their beginnings can't be found
And neither can their ends.

They always travel in a group,
A churning, turning ante-troop
Of canterloping Anteloop,
Both enemies and friends.

So please do not get in the way
When Anteloop come out to play,
Or you'll be dizzy for a day
And maybe get the bends.

THE MUSTANKS

From out of the West since it was won
We've cow and horse herds by the ton.
But Mustank herds? Why, we have none,
Though Mustanks are in town.

They gallop by in thunderous herds
And frighten children, men, and birds;
And for their smell there are no words,
When Mustanks are in town.

So if you see a cloud go by,
And hear a wild, forsaken cry,
Just hold your nose — or you'll know why:
DHU MUSTAGS ARH IN DOWN.

12

THE BUMPLE BEE

How very like the Bumple Bee
To tumple to the floor
When he has had too much for tea
(He always asks for more).

He eats his meals so messily,
(He's not like you or I)
And lets the little pieces all
Go crumpling on his tie.

His little buzz, it mumples so,
His clothes are all a-jumple,
His tummy always rumples on,
That common little Bumple.

THE SPRINKLER SPANIEL

The Sprinkler Spaniel always runs
In through the open door
And shakes its soggy head and makes
A mess upon my floor.

I do despise that canine cuss,
I do indeed abhor
The soggy tracks, the muddy rug,
The mess upon my floor.

THE RHINOCERWORSE

His mother is a meany,
His father is a bum,
His sister is a nasty louse,
His brother is a crumb.
Yet still, he could be better
And renounce the family curse.
But he is twice as bad as they —
He is Rhinocerworse.

16

THE WHYSEL

If you ever meet a Whysel
He will question you to death.
He will sit upon your tummy.
He won't let you get your breath.

He will ask, but you can't answer
When he's sitting on you so,
Yet he won't get up and leave until
You've told him all you know.

So if you meet a Whysel
I'm afraid you've met your match,
For your breath you won't be catching
If a Whysel you should catch.

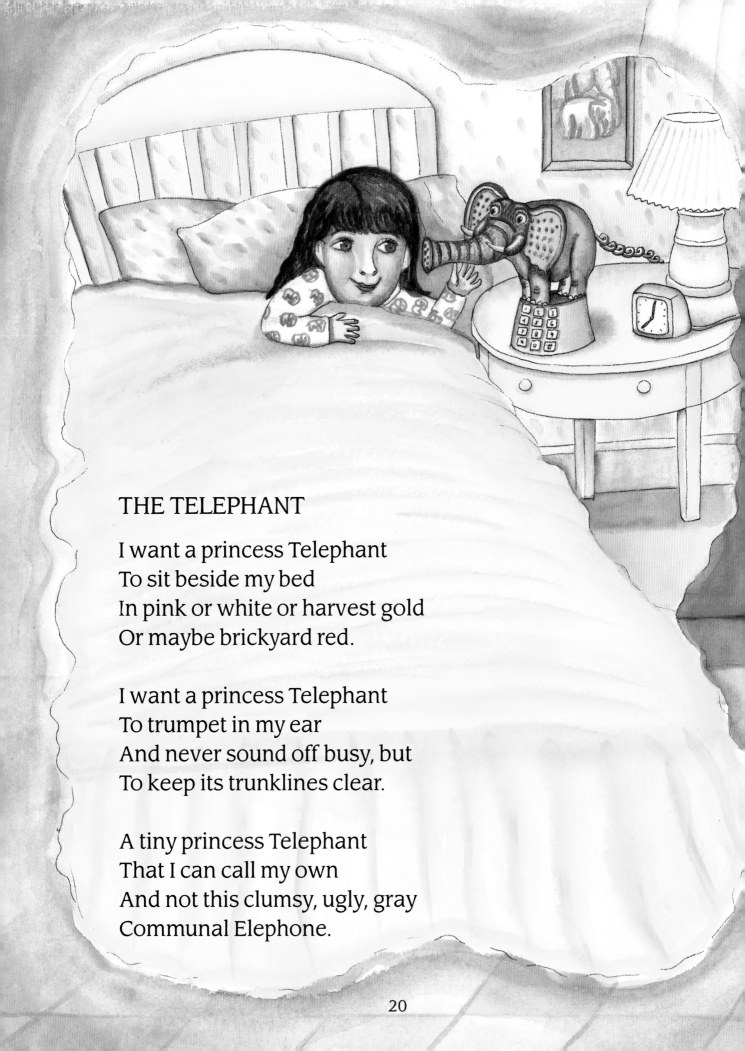

THE TELEPHANT

I want a princess Telephant
To sit beside my bed
In pink or white or harvest gold
Or maybe brickyard red.

I want a princess Telephant
To trumpet in my ear
And never sound off busy, but
To keep its trunklines clear.

A tiny princess Telephant
That I can call my own
And not this clumsy, ugly, gray
Communal Elephone.

THE HIPPOPOTANOOSE

Oh, what is fat and comes in coils
Prepared for cowboy use?
The newest thing in lariats:
The Hippopotanoose.

Its only drawback is its size,
For hang it on your saddle
And any normal quarterhorse
Will be inclined to waddle.

But throw it round a running steer,
Or round a big stampede,
The Hippopotanoose will fill
A cowpoke's every need.

THE MOCKIT BIRD

The Xerox of the forest,
The mimic of the glen,
Sometimes it sounds like oysters,
Sometimes it sounds like men,
Sometimes it sings like rabbits,
Sometimes it growls like mice,
Sometimes it laughs like apples,
Sometimes it coughs like dice.
It's very hard to find one,
Far worse to make one stay,
For found, it sounds like robbers
And, silent, steals away.

THE GRIZZLY BARE

The Grizzly Bare
Don't wear
No clothes.

Inside his lair
He's fair-
Ly froze.

So have a care
And share
Your hose

So Grizzly Bare
Can air
His toes.

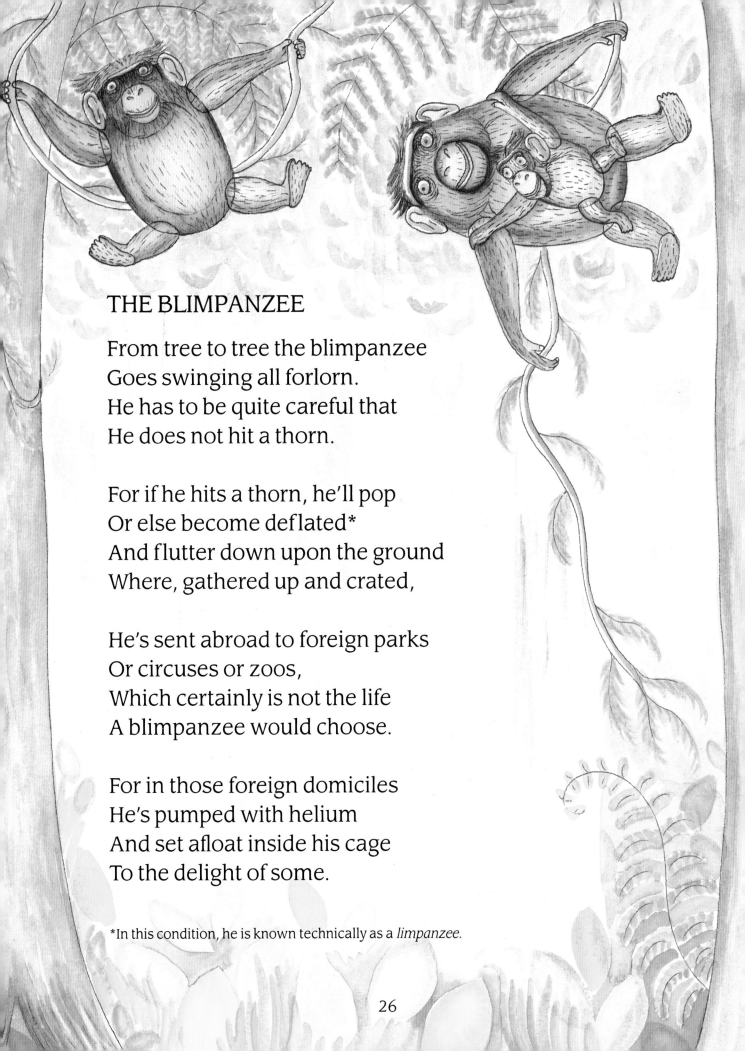

THE BLIMPANZEE

From tree to tree the blimpanzee
Goes swinging all forlorn.
He has to be quite careful that
He does not hit a thorn.

For if he hits a thorn, he'll pop
Or else become deflated*
And flutter down upon the ground
Where, gathered up and crated,

He's sent abroad to foreign parks
Or circuses or zoos,
Which certainly is not the life
A blimpanzee would choose.

For in those foreign domiciles
He's pumped with helium
And set afloat inside his cage
To the delight of some.

*In this condition, he is known technically as a *limpanzee*.

THE CAMELEPHANT

The Camelephant's a lumpy cuss,
His nose, it is truncated.
His humps are hidden under hair,
His tail is long and plaited.

He cannot cross a desert waste,
He cannot cross a jungle.
It's clear that evolution has,
In his case, made a bungle.

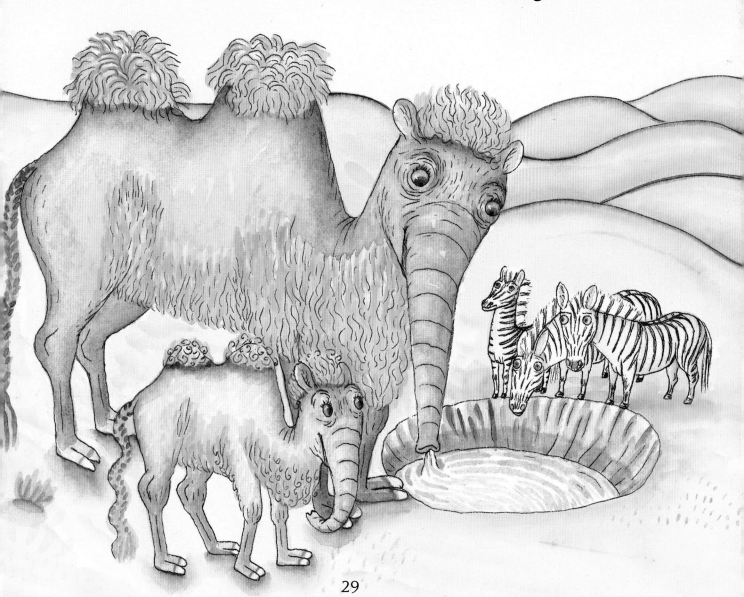

29

THE GIRAFT

If you're out in the ocean, afloat on the deep,
With the sharks making straight for your craft,
Simply close your eyes tightly and whistle a shrill
S.O.S. for the nearest Giraft.

If you plan to be going away on a cruise
And you find your lifeboats understaffed,
Do not give it a thought, simply whistle a tune
That will call on the nearest Giraft.

30

For they sail very swiftly, can outpace a sub,
And their periscope necks fore and aft
Let them keep a sharp eye on the ocean so no
One can sneak up behind a Giraft.

I have rowed many miles and have sailed quite a few,
And on none of those trips have I laughed,
For my travels all filled me with fear and with dread
Till I learned of the friendly Giraft.

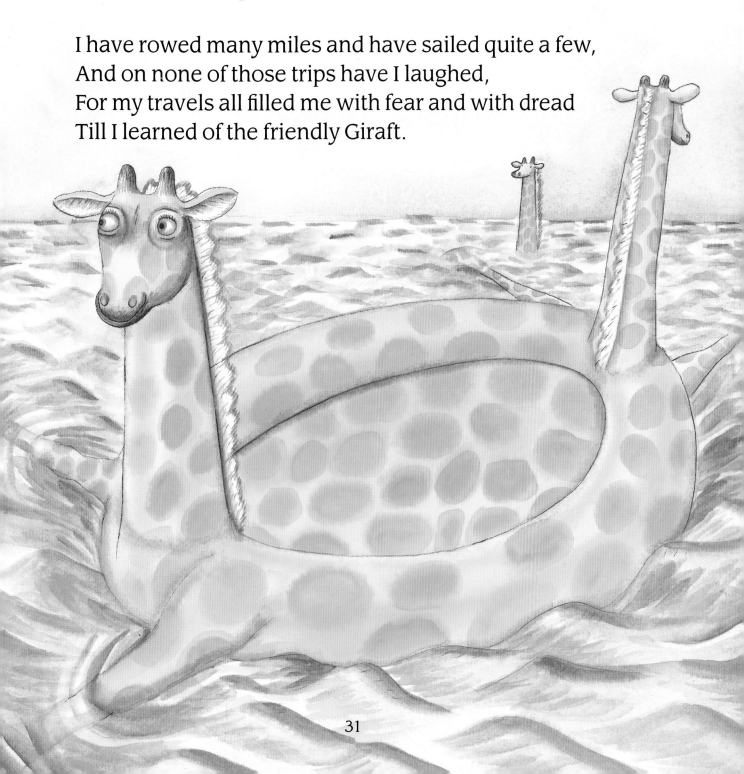

THE RAGGIT

A tear of ear, a wisp of tail,
The raggit's caught upon a rail.
A thread of skin, a rip of hair,
A shred of hop, no longer there.